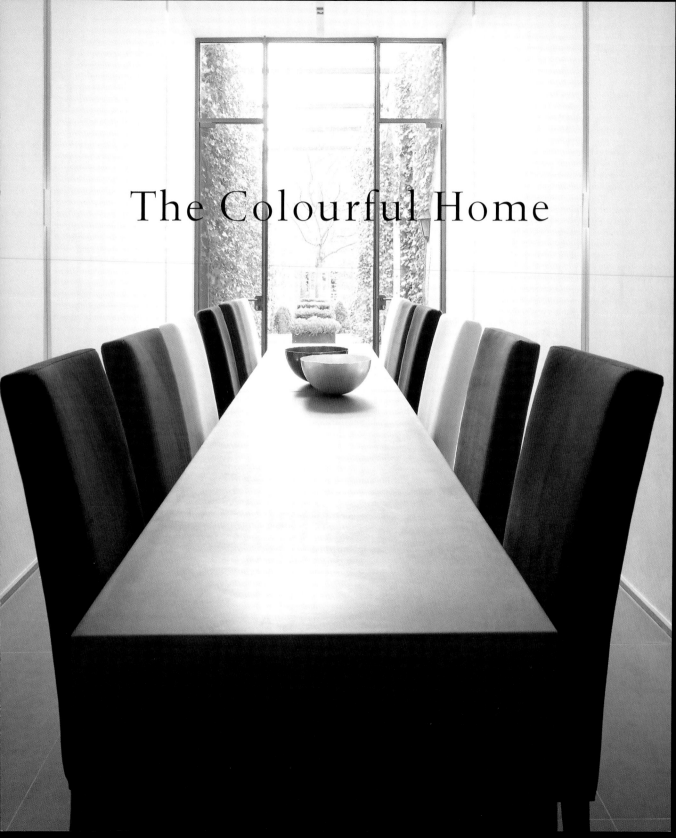

The Colourful Home

The Colourful Home

CONFIDENT AND CREATIVE COLOUR SCHEMES FOR EVERY ROOM

Vinny Lee

jacqui small

First published in 2010 by Jacqui Small LLP,
7 Greenland Street, London NW1 0ND

PUBLISHER Jacqui Small
EDITORIAL MANAGER Kerenza Swift
DESIGNER Maggie Town
EDITOR Sian Parkhouse
PICTURE RESEARCHER Nadine Bazar
PRODUCTION Peter Colley

ISBN 978 1906417 19 2

A catalogue record for this book is
available from the British Library.

2012 2011 2010
10 9 8 7 6 5 4 3 2 1

Printed in China

contents

Every home should have a sense of place. This can be created by the use of colour, the architectural features and the arrangement of furnishings, but of these three ingredients colour will make the most impact. Colour is a relatively simple thing to add or to subtract, and as well as being used to heighten and accent it can be useful

in remedial ways, changing negative spaces into positive ones. A coat of primrose paint will transform a dark windowless passageway into a light and inviting hall; red-toned colours can make a large space warmer and more intimate.

Colour can be used to create a scheme that has depth and interest as well as expressing something of the personality of the owner, and personality and individuality are an important part of making an apartment or house into a home. A series of blank white rooms is neither comforting nor relaxing, whereas a colourful home can give enjoyment and pleasure, with spaces that stimulate, relax and are memorable. Don't be intimidated by the prospect of using colour: it doesn't need to be bold to make an impact; subtle shades can be as effective in creating a mood or atmosphere. Play with colour, enjoy it – the combinations are infinite.

Vinny Lee

OPPOSITE TOP A mixed palette of colours and objects can be unified by a background or wall of a single strong colour. Dominant shades and colours such as terracotta, russet red or black will allow the colours of the objects and fabrics to be seen but not to overpower.

OPPOSITE BELOW Brightly coloured accessories and flowers can be used to contrast against plain and dark coloured backgrounds. These small items can be changed so that the mood and appearance of the room can be easily updated.

THIS PAGE A white or neutral background will accommodate any colour, including this natural palette of soft brown and tan shades, but to prevent the scheme being dull add texture and pattern.

the psychology
of colour

Every day we are surrounded by colour which, in its many hues and combinations, stimulates us visually and emotionally. Colour can be used to attract or warn us, to highlight things or to make them blend into the background. Over the centuries colour has been investigated and analysed to help our understanding of its qualities and effects. In the late 17th century Sir Isaac Newton demonstrated that a prism could split white light into a spectrum of colours. In 1824 French chemist Michel Eugene Chevreul noticed colours often looked different when placed beside each other. But perhaps the person who had the most direct effect on the way we work with colour today was Johannes Itten, who taught at the Bauhaus in 1920s Germany. Itten identified 'Colour Chords' with three primary colours and twelve intermediary hues, all of which we look at later in this chapter.

A century after Newton's discovery Johann Goethe studied the psychological effect of colour and noted that blue gives a feeling of coolness whereas yellow has a warming effect. His work was expanded by Rudolf Steiner. Their observations are used today to design interiors that influence the way we work and relax.

The effects of colour are more than decorative, they also play an important role in the way we feel and respond to our surroundings, so choosing the right palette for your rooms is a vital part of creating a home.

TOP LEFT Some colours are associated with places; lavender blue is linked to Provence not only because fields of lavender are grown there, but also because it is used to paint the doors and shutters of the houses in the area.

TOP RIGHT Against a plain backdrop a single area of contrasting colour will become a focal point. Here the red cushions on the curved chair give a 'wow' factor to an otherwise white and understated setting.

BOTTOM LEFT Warm colours give an impression of heat and are useful in cold, north-facing rooms, but colour test an area of wall to see that it remains bright, rather than taking on a sludgy hue.

BOTTOM RIGHT Green is regarded as a fresh, youthful and invigorating colour and is sometimes used in a bathroom to give a feeling of enthusiasm and brightness to preparations at the start of the day.

PREVIOUS PAGES Brilliant reds are said to 'vibrate' but this effect can be lessened by using a shade such as white or black, or a neutralizing tone of dark blue, brown or grey.

ABOVE Red is useful as a highlight colour and can be used to bring a feeling of warmth to a cool room or as a focal point to an otherwise plainly decorated space. Red is also the colour of warning, so could be used to convey the fact that an area, such as an oven or grill, may be hot or dangerous.

RIGHT A red bath instantly gives the impression of warmth and enveloping comfort, and with contemporary synthetic materials it is possible to have bathroom furniture in a rainbow selection of shades and colours.

PURE AND PRIMARY

In interior design terms the three main colour chords, as described by Johannes Itten, are the primary colours and the intermediary hues are divided into secondary and tertiary colours.

Primary colours are most vivid when placed next to each other, which is useful when creating a commercial sign or logo, but may prove over-powering in a domestic setting. They are strong colours and should be used in moderation. But let us start with the three primary colours and their qualities:

RED

Red is a hot and emotional colour linked to fire, blood, war and danger. It is also associated with energy, passion and desire. Exposure to this colour is said to induce physical changes, such as speeding up metabolism, increasing respiration rate and raising blood pressure; it can also help to improve poor circulation and energy levels. Red is a highly visible colour so is used to warn of hazards and in signals such as traffic and brake lights. Although red brings drama and excitement to a room, too much pure or undiluted red can promote feelings of overheating and anxiety, so some care should be taken.

Historically red has been used in large cold rooms to bring a feeling of warmth; it is also a colour favoured for the walls of galleries and museums such as the Dulwich Picture Gallery and The Royal Academy of Arts in London's Piccadilly. Paintings framed in black or gold and sculpture in white or grey marble are enhanced by a background in this colour.

In a hallway or entrance area, where natural light is often limited, a red rug or runner is always a welcoming sight – the red will draw a person into the building and make an immediate impression.

Yellow and white makes a fresh, bright combination that benefits from being lit by natural light. Some shades of yellow may become dull and sometimes take on a green hue if viewed in artificial light – to avoid this try daylight-quality bulbs or use the yellow in a room occupied mainly during the day.

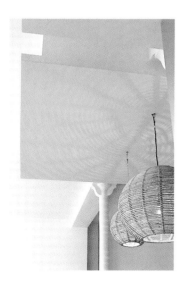

YELLOW

Like red, this is another 'hot' colour so any shade with an element of yellow in its composition will add a feeling of brightness and warmth. Yellow, being the colour of the sun, is said to promote cheerfulness and muscle energy. It is also associated with joy, happiness, intellect and energy, but if used on large areas it can be over-stimulating.

Yellow is one of the colours most affected by the light source by which it is seen. A shade of yellow seen in daylight may look bright and fresh, but will appear sludgy and dull in artificial light, so always test yellow paint and fabrics in various lights before including them in a scheme.

Because yellow is a cheerful and spontaneous colour it isn't suitable as a main colour for an office or business environment. Yellow is also a colour avoided when advertising expensive products, especially to men, because they tend to regard it as a childish tone.

ABOVE The perceived 'heat' of yellow can be cooled if used in conjunction with white or black. Panels of yellow can give the impression of radiant light or, if used behind an electric source, will reflect some of the emitted light, giving it a more yellow hue.

RIGHT This yellow Perspex door allows light to travel through it, but the resulting light will take on a hint of the colour. Looking through the door to the study beyond gives the impression that the room itself is bathed in golden sunlight, even on a dull or overcast day.

15

BLUE

This is classified as a cool colour because it reminds people of water and the sky; it is regarded as being beneficial to the mind and body and has the effect of slowing human metabolism and blood pressure and producing a feeling of calm. Blue is also traditionally the colour of masculinity.

The qualities that blue is said to represent include piety, sincerity, stability and cleanliness. At the White House in Washington there is an oval Blue Room where the President of the United States receives guests; the colour presumably calms the guests before meeting the President. It is also a colour associated with homes in Mediterranean or tropical locations; its cooling effect can be seen at Frida Kahlo and Diego Rivera's Blue House in Coyoacán, where the vivid blue counteracts the Mexican heat and intense light.

Blue suppresses bright and warm colours such as yellow and red, so be careful about using it in kitchens without a good supply of light, because it can affect the way raw ingredients and cooked dishes appear. But it is a good colour to choose for a bathroom, with its watery connection and fresh feel, or a child's bedroom, where the calming effect can be beneficial. But blue should be used with care – too much can create a feeling of coldness, especially in the northern hemisphere where the light is less warm, and it can be a depressive colour and create a feeling of loneliness.

ABOVE This tonal arrangement of accessories in various shades of green set against a green wall make a pleasant vignette, which focuses the eye on the shapes, textures and finishes of the objects as well as the thematic colour.

ABOVE RIGHT With its association with vegetables, plants and fruit, green is a colour compatible with the kitchen and cooking. In Mediterranean countries, such as southern France and Italy, green ceramic tableware is popular, and provides a complementary background to crisps salads, tomatoes and other brightly coloured foodstuffs.

LEFT With its leafy outlook and indoor topiary this room already has close links to nature, but the use of green in the blind and upholstery emphasizes this proximity and accentuates the colour of the foliage.

SECONDARY COLOURS

The secondary colours are green, orange and purple, which are formed by mixing equal quantities of the primaries. Therefore: yellow + blue = green; yellow + red = orange and blue + red = purple.

Secondary colours are often regarded as being more interesting and versatile than the three primaries colours because they have a more complex composition. Also, they do not give the same direct sense of urgency or immediateness, so can be easier to work with.

GREEN

This is the colour of nature and symbolizes freshness, abundance, harmony and growth; it is a restful colour and is also said to have healing powers. Because of its association with nature many of the names given to shades of green are sourced from there, for example apple, olive, moss and pistachio.

The calming and restful aspects of the colour can be demonstrated firsthand in the 'Green Room' that is often found in television studios and theatres. This was a space originally painted green to give the actors' eyes a rest from the glare of the stage lights, but these days it refers to a room where guests go to relax before going on stage or on air.

ORANGE

This is a vigorous and vital colour, combining the energy of red and the joy of yellow. It represents readiness, enthusiasm and happiness and is also a stimulating colour which registers as being hot and vibrant to the human eye. When used in conjunction with red it adds to the overall heat of the scheme, whereas if added to a palette based on a more neutral range of browns and taupe, it contributes warmth and interest.

Orange, like yellow, is said to be a saturated colour and also vibrant, which means that it 'glows'. Philosopher and academic Rudolf Steiner noted that visually these 'hot' colours are most intense in the centre but appear to diminish as they span outwards. He said 'Yellow, from its intrinsic nature, wants to become weaker and weaker at its edges'; this is especially true if you place a panel of yellow or orange next to white – where the two abut the colour will appear to dissolve or melt into the white.

In decorative terms orange is a colour that is not often used for a whole scheme; it is more frequently used as a highlight or accent colour (see pages 46–49). It was popular in the 1960s and '70s in psychedelic and Pop Art prints and designs and is often used as a base for gold leaf or gold paint, to give depth and intensity to the uppermost layer.

LEFT Squares of different shades of orange make this wall less hot and imposing than if it was in a single strong hue. Orange is regarded as a contemporary colour and here, with a classic wing chair and a framed portrait, it updates the room.

RIGHT By using a softer yellow shade of orange on the recessed area the intensity of the other walls is diluted. The room is also carefully furnished so that there is space within the visually 'hot' environment.

LEFT Purple can be a
sombre colour so to prevent
it being oppressive it is best
used in small quantities
and against a lighter
background. Here chairs
and footstools set on a
white tiled floor become a
feature of the room.

RIGHT Purple is a colour
associated with luxury and
opulence so this finely
detailed, elegant period
chair and footstool are
appropriately upholstered
in a rich shade of the colour.

PURPLE

As a mix of two colours, purple takes aspects from both; it has the stability
of blue counteracted by the unmistakable energy of red. It is used to convey
an impression of wealth, nobility and luxury, but it also has links with magic
and mystery as well as creativity and independence.

Purple is a colour that owes its rise in popularity to the discovery in 1856
by William Henry Perkin of the synthetic dye aniline purple. Previously it
was a difficult colour to source – during Roman times it was extracted from
a shellfish and because of its rarity and cost was worn only by royalty and the
nobility. Natural purple dyes obtained from berries and roots quickly faded
or turned to brown so were an unsatisfactory source for strong tones.

Purple is said to be a good colour with which to decorate a room or space
where contemplation or meditation is to take place, but because in its pure
form it is a dominant, intense colour it is best used in panels or as a feature
colour. It is also a colour associated with Bohemians and those of an artistic
temperament and may be found in the homes of painters, writers and actors.

In a light, bright room with a wall of floor-to-ceiling glass and a pale-coloured, light-reflecting floor, the black upholstered sofa and rug balance the intensity of the natural light and whiteness.

BLACK, WHITE AND GREY

Black and white are technically shades rather than colours, and when used together in their purest forms they create a monochrome scheme which can be dramatic and is always sophisticated.

White is associated with light, innocence, goodness and purity; it is also the representative of perfection and cleanliness. Expressions such as 'pure as the driven snow' sum up the impression given by brilliant white.

On the other hand, black has many negative connotations; it is linked to death, evil, mystery, power and formality. But it also denotes elegance. You only have to think in fashion terms of the innate glamour of the 'little black dress' and a black tie event; it is the colour that is said to make people look slimmer and objects and furniture more streamlined.

White, whether on a painted wall or in textiles will lighten a room and appear to brighten other colours used in conjunction with it, while black is a good contrast colour because it emphasizes and accentuates other more

LEFT This monochrome scheme balances clinical white and cool polished steel with the grounding effect of black. The use of black on the lower units is practical because it doesn't show scuffs and marks as much as a white façade or door.

BELOW White is a high-maintenance shade and in any scheme it must be kept pristine, therefore china and plates on display will need to be washed regularly and upholstery fabrics laundered and pressed.

vivid colours. Black may also be used architecturally to create a feeling of perspective and depth and as a background it will seem to diminish, making the painted area appear smaller and further away, so emphasizing space.

When blended into another colour black will darken and dull, while white will make it pale and less dominant. This darkening and lightening of a colour creates what is called a shade or hue and may be used, as part of the same family of colour, to extend the range of a decorative scheme.

GREY

When black and white are mixed together they form grey and when grey (which like black and white is a shade rather than a colour) is added to a colour it reduces the purity and intensity of the colour, making it a softer more muted shade. Grey is popular with contemporary designers and is often found in natural materials or in artificial shades that reference them by name, for example stone, slate and charcoal.

Grey is a perfect foil for intense colours such as shocking pink and cobalt blue, and has a natural affinity with metals such as chrome, silver and steel. You can also have 'warm' and 'cool' greys – the warmer shades are tinged with red while the cooler versions have more blue in their make-up.

Certain shades of grey have sludgy overtones that can be interpreted as dusty or grimy, so they are not suitable for use in rooms where food is prepared, and it is best to avoid a grey scheme in a windowless room or one where there is little natural light, because it can create a dull, depressing feel.

Dove grey is a calm and
restful colour and when
teamed with white, which
alleviates the 'dull' aspect
of the shade, it can be
used to create an elegant
and sophisticated scheme.

NEUTRALS

Neutrals are soft, undemanding shades that provide an off-white background to many schemes. Neutral colours are useful as a means to set off brilliant accessories and vibrant patterned wallpapers, but they can be used in conjunction with bright colours as well as used wholly on their own.

Neutral colours tend to have names such as oatmeal, magnolia and ecru, chalk and parchment, denoting that within the overall background of white there is just a hint of another colour – the merest hint of yellow, pink, beige, grey or blue. These colours may also be divided into warm whites and cool whites – going back to the primary colours where red and yellow or any hint of those colours makes a secondary or tertiary colour or associated shade appear warmer, while the opposite is true for anything with a blue base.

There are a myriad neutral shades, or shades of white that provide a subtle contrast or an undemanding background to a scheme. They are useful where pure white would be too harsh a contrast and in a space where a subtle touch of specific warmth or coolness is desired.

ABOVE A coat or two of a pale or natural-coloured paint can be used to transform a faded wooden floor or an aged piece of furniture. The ground work of stripping off varnish and sanding is essential for a good result.

LEFT Because of the off-white nature of neutral tones they have the effect of making white seem even more brilliant, but be careful that the brightness of the white doesn't make the neutral colour look sludgy or dirty.

OPPOSITE Soft or neutral colours are undemanding and convey a feeling of tranquillity, so they are invaluable in bedroom schemes.

BLENDED TONES

This is a term that describes colours derived from two sources, firstly those taken from the tertiary colour palette. These are the colours in the next stage of development beyond the secondary cycle.

Tertiary colours are created by mixing more of one primary colour and less of another so, for example instead of the half and half mix of the secondary cycle purple, the tertiary palette will have a purple that is more red – a raspberry shade – made up of two parts red and one part blue. There can also be a blueberry purple made up of two parts blue with one part red, therefore putting the accent on the blue end of the spectrum. These colours are also referred to as harmonious because, like a chord in music, they have the same key note or colour and are therefore compatible.

The other category of blended tones is the darker and lighter shades, or tonal colours. These are created by adding white, black or grey to the main colour. For example, by adding white to raspberry pink you would create a pastel pink. By adding grey you will create a smoky or dusky pink, or by adding black you would make a grey with a warm pink undertone.

The tertiary colours and darker and lighter tones enable you to create a family of colours, often referred to as a basic palette. This palette or range of colours is connected by a common base or primary colour. For example, pink, brown and dark red all share the common 'ancestry' of red, although in different quantities, so they are compatible, as are yellow, green and brown because they share a common yellow 'ancestry'.

The palette of harmonious and tonal shades allows you to work around your chosen key colour. If you were to decorate a whole room in a single colour it could be boring and overpowering, whereas by adding a selection of these blended colours you achieve a personal look with variety and interest.

THE WARM END OF THE COLOUR SPECTRUM

Shades that have an element of red in their composition are said to be warm because they seem to radiate or emit an impression of heat.

LIGHT RED is said to represent the feelings of joy, passion and love. At its brightest and most intense this colour may have a hint of yellow in its

ABOVE This wall colour has a strong element of red in its composition, but mixing it with yellow, and a small but calming element of grey, makes it less vibrant than a true orange.

composition which will add to its perceived 'radiant' heat. These bright reds come under such names as scarlet, pillar box, poppy and firecracker. The French 20th-century artist renowned for his use of colour, Henri Matisse, painted flowers, fabric and a woman to dramatic effect against a background of brilliant red in *The Dessert: Harmony in Red (The Red Room)*. He advised: 'Seek out the strongest colour effect possible.'

LEFT Shades of pink that are blended with blue merge into the lavender spectrum. As a colour lavender, as with the flower and its perfume, is said to be calming and restful, so is appropriate for use in a bedroom.

ABOVE Pink has been a popular colour throughout history since the Romans first made a purple-red dye from the cochineal beetle. It can be found in many delicate and subtle shades as well as hot and vibrant tones.

PINK The colour of romance and friendship and often linked to feminine qualities, pink is created by blending red with white and shades of it are described by evocative words such as rose, blush, blossom or candy floss. Too much sugary or pastel pink can be cloying, but it is a useful highlight colour (see Accent Colour pages 46–49) and its 'sweetness' can be reduced or controlled when teamed with grey, black or brown.

A colour scheme for a room may be inspired by an object or artwork. Here a dramatic circular picture provides the palette of pastel pink for the walls, rose pink and red for the rug and black for the armchair and other accessories.

This brown panel is harmonious with the overall scheme because its composition consists of both red and a small amount of black.

OPPOSITE TOP A wholly brown interior gives a comfortable and enveloping feel to a room and is often used in a study, den or small sitting room where the feeling of relaxation is a priority.

OPPOSITE BELOW Transparent, coloured or tinted panels and room dividers provide not only a screen but can also affect the light that passes through them, creating a wash of colour across a room or wall.

BELOW The choice of red for this brick-patterned feature plays on the shapes and colours of traditional house bricks.

DARK RED represents a sense of vigour, willpower and leadership. This colour may have an element of dark blue or black in its composition combined with primary red. This shade is often marketed under such names as bordeaux, burgundy and claret, as in the classic wines, or cardinal red, which carries suggestions of those aspects of leadership and power I referred to. Another well-known dark red is referred to as Eating Room Red and, as the name suggests, it has been used through the centuries to decorate the walls of dining rooms. At the home of the late Finnish Prime Minster Carl Gustaf Mannerheim the dining room is painted in plum red and grey. He is said to have chosen the scheme because 'red is good for digestion and grey stimulates conversation'.

REDDISH BROWN These tones convey warmth, security and maturity; many of the names used to describe them are derived from earth pigments or

location where they are found, for example terracotta and Etruscan red, or from fruits such as russet, which reflects the colour of the mature apple skin.

BROWN is an earthy colour that indicates stability. Brown falls into two categories: the more utilitarian shades such as ox tail, raw umber and burnt oak; and the more alluring with names such as nut-brown, spice, chestnut, cocoa and chocolate.

DARK ORANGE These rich autumnal tones evoke images of ripeness and richness. Colours include bronze, tarnished copper and amber, and when mixed with white they create coral tones.

RED-ORANGE describes hot, vibrant colours that represent desire, sexual passion and action. When mixed with white they produce apricot tones, but in their unadulterated form they are classified as fireball, clementine, glow, zest and flame.

PRIMROSE YELLOW is a happy colour that stands for intellect, freshness and joy. Many related shades take their names from flowers, from the paler jasmine and buttercup to the richer sunflower and daffodil. With a hint of brown, they become more honey toned, and eventually ochre.

LIME GREEN Add a little blue to primrose yellow and you will discover lime green, a bright, zesty colour that provides an eye-catching background to black and chrome, or colourful accessories.

RIGHT This bright, fresh primrose yellow feature wall gives warmth and interest to the wholly white kitchen and also creates a visual barrier between the 'working' part of the room and the relaxing zone on the other side.

LEFT This fresh green cabinet and the pale green door and frames sit comfortably against the pale blue wall because the green is fashioned from blue and yellow, and for this shade a proportion of white.

OLIVE GREEN is a muted sludgy shade which was traditionally the colour of peace. It is a useful in a natural palette using wood, brown, ochre and yellow, but it is worth trying out a colour swatch test in both natural and artificial light, because this colour may look predominantly green by day but become muddy brown when viewed in electric light.

DARK GREEN is associated with ambition, greed and jealousy. Racing green is a shade found on classic cars, especially British ones. Forest, as the name suggests, is the colour of a canopy of leafy trees, and bottle green is the colour of wine bottles. This colour is strong but can be used to dramatic effect in a candle-lit dining room or other areas used mostly in the evening.

LEFT Olive green has a measure of brown in its make-up, which softens the zesty nature of its more pure family member in the secondary band of colours. This makes olive a more suitable shade for 'restful' zones.

RIGHT Muted greens such as celadon and light jade were found in the ceramics and carvings at the court of the Chinese Imperial family – to this day these shades are regarded as precious and fine.

LEFT This chequerboard floor combines blues and green, which link in with the pale turquoise wall colour that has elements of both colours in its composition.

OPPOSITE The pattern and quantity of the curtain fabric, which is also used on the upholstered footboard, and the red in the cushion and striped fabric of the chaise longue, balance the icy coolness of the aqua walls, so that the appearance of the room is fresh rather than cold.

BELOW The simplicity of the tongue and groove panelled wood staircase is endorsed by the used of a white-based, blue-green paint. The effect is clean and understated.

COOL SHADES

Shades that have blue in their composition are said to be cool, but these colours often have a chameleon quality which makes them change depending on other colours used with them or the light in which they are seen. Cool blue daylight, common in the northern hemisphere in winter, will enhance their blueness, but green accessories will bring out the green element. AQUA is a green-blue with a hint of yellow in its composition. Aqua is said to promote emotional healing and to give a feeling of protection. In its darker variations it is the colour found in peacock feathers and in its paler tone the icy coolness of glaciers.

LIGHT BLUE is the colour of tranquillity and associated with masculinity. This fresh and attractive colour is found in varying shades such as powder blue, wedgwood, bluebell or baby blue.

DARK BLUE is said to be the colour of knowledge and power and in one of its incarnations is known as Oxford blue, the colour worn by the athletes of Oxford University. Delft blue, a crisp rich tone, is found on tiles and takes its name from the Dutch town where they were originally made. In its black-rich deepest tone dark blue is often named midnight.

ABOVE Light blue is a tranquil colour, therefore suitable for a bedroom. Teamed with white it also gives an impression of freshness and airiness, which can be beneficial in a small or confined space.

LEFT A random mix of mosaic tiles in varying shades of blue and grey are reminiscent of dappled water, which is an appropriate wall finish for a walk-in shower room.

OPPOSITE In the mid-1700s potter Josiah Wedgwood used pale blue as a background to his neo-classical inspired ceramics, which featured applied white silhouetted figures; since then the combination of pale blue and white has been a classic scheme.

OPPOSITE Light purple is a colour whose popularity comes in and out of fashion; it has its fans and its detractors. It is a colour that has an affinity with dark woods such as mahogany and cherry wood, which have, like purple, a quantity of red in their make-up.

ABOVE RIGHT As with pale pink, too much light purple can be cloying, so the amount of uninterrupted wall space in this colour should be limited. Here a padded headboard in a deeper shade breaks up the flow of the pale shade.

RIGHT Purple and black is a strong and striking combination and when combined with chrome these shades can be used to create Art Deco period style. The brightness and shine of chrome balances the depth of the dark purple and black. In a bedroom, crisp white bed linen will also alleviate the darker aspects of the scheme.

LIGHT PURPLE is a shade associated with romance and nostalgia. Many shades are named after flowers, such as lavender, lilac, wisteria and hyacinth, as well as the semi-precious stone amethyst.

DARK PURPLE has royal connotations of wealth and solidarity, but it may also be connected with feelings of sadness. These rich shades are often available under the names of winter pansy, regal and imperial purple.

ACCENT COLOURS

In decorating terms the colour used in the largest quantity or in the greatest proportion is classified as the dominant or ground colour and the colours used in smaller areas are referred to as subdominant. Accent colours are those that cover a small area but offer a contrast because of their intensity or 'opposition' to the dominant colour.

Accent colours that come under the classification of contrasting colours are found at the opposing side of the colour wheel or spectrum to the main colour. For example, if your palette is predominantly blue then the opposite or contrast colour will be orange; for yellow it is purple; and for green, red.

Contrasting colours can be used to vary the mood of a scheme. For example, in a cool blue room a fabric wall panel or accessories in orange will warm the general appearance. If a purple-themed room is in danger of becoming too mellow and moody then an injection of yellow will lighten and brighten the place, but with red and green make sure the balance

ABOVE LEFT The accent colours of rust and olive green were chosen because they are muted and part of a 'natural' palette that includes brown, which is one of the dominant colours in this room.

ABOVE RIGHT The panel of deep purple adds a feeling of gravitas and seriousness to this office area; if the wall had been all white the initial impression would have been of a blank and uninteresting room.

RIGHT A single, slim vibrant pink cushion breaks up the muted scheme of grey, black and brown. This small but effective flash of colour shows how much impact a well-chosen accent colour can have on the appearance of a room.

LEFT The muted softness of this mainly pale and grey scheme is given an uplift by the introduction of a few vivid, yellow accessories. With accent colours the impact can be effectively made with just a few vibrant pieces.

doesn't tip too far and that there are variations on the 'contrast' colour. If a scheme comprising red and green becomes too evenly balanced or if the red and green are of equal vividness or intensity there is a danger of the 'traffic light effect' where the colours bounce off each other and create an uneasy and restless environment. To avoid this ensure that the accent colour is used sparingly and in a variety of tones.

An accent colour may also be a tonal variation, which provides a subtle and sophisticated contrast. For instance, in a room that is predominantly pale blue a single wall or chimney breast of dark blue will alleviate the monotony of the scheme. You may also use a tonal variation to alter the balance or appearance of a room   if your scheme is mainly focused on a hot red-orange you could introduce a panel of a more yellow shade to lessen the intensity of the red and emphasize the yellowness of the main colour.

In a white room any colour can be used as an accent but make sure that the colour is picked up elsewhere in furniture or accessories otherwise it may look isolated rather than an intended feature. To link the accent colour you may include it in fabrics, such as a colour in tweed upholstery or printed textile. The colour may also be carried through in glassware or ceramics.

The rule is 'less is more' with accent colours. If you introduce too many or too much they merge into the overall scheme, whereas a small amount will have a greater and more notable effect.

the elements

A home is made up of various elements, such as surfaces, furnishings and accessories and each one of these can be used to introduce or add colour – but even the most spontaneous colour scheme needs planning if it is to achieve an agreeable environment, one where you feel comfortable as well as interested and involved. For those who are wary of committing to a strong colour scheme the easiest and safest way to start is with a small amount – for example, a single piece of colourful furniture, a brightly toned rug or a scattering of jewel-coloured cushions. Once you have become acclimatized to this introductory amount of 'adjustable' colour – meaning that you can move it around the room and add or subtract from it – you may feel that you are ready for the next step, to add a larger 'fixed' surface of colour, such as a feature wall or a large carpet.

When you are ready to decorate with colour turn your attention to the more complex issue of achieving balance. This involves weighing up the intensity and volume of colour in your room and offsetting an overly 'hot' scheme with 'cooling' elements, or visa versa. It is also important to counter blocks of solid colour with areas of pattern, as well as textured surfaces with smooth, and hard with soft.

Achieving the right balance and mix of elements, surfaces and finishes adds to the complexity of the overall scheme and therefore its depth and interest – all of which gives your scheme personality and longevity.

TOP LEFT This predominantly monochrome scheme is lifted with a highlight of bright red cushions that draws the attention to the head of the bed and the painting above.

TOP RIGHT Upholstered sofas tend to be large and notable pieces of furniture, so the fabric and trimmings will have a strong impact on your overall scheme.

BOTTOM LEFT A bright rug or mat is a useful way to break up a large expanse of single-coloured flooring; it can also focus the eye on a particular piece of furniture.

BOTTOM RIGHT Unusual pieces of furniture, such as these contemporary, low-armed chairs, will stand out against a neutral background if upholstered in a strong single colour.

PREVIOUS PAGES By using fresh, bright green as a highlight colour the link is clearly made between this room and the garden seen through the large picture window; the colour enhances the indoor-outdoor aspect of the location.

OPPOSITE A rough-hewn stone wall works well in a rustic or warehouse setting. Both the deep grey and the lighter orange-brown shades in the stone are reflected in the colours of the steel frame and wooden treads of the staircase. The polished wooden floor helps to soften the overall appearance of the room.

ABOVE RIGHT Stone and brick come in a variety of tones and shades, which create an innate and subtle pattern or decorative effect. This works well as a background to plain upholstered furniture.

WALLS

Although many contemporary homes and apartments have large expanses of glass, solid walls still provide a major part of the internal structure of any home, and are a blank canvas on which solid colour or various designs or pattern can be applied with paper or paint. Walls can be left plain as a statement in their own right or act as a background on which paintings, artworks or photographs can be displayed.

NATURAL MATERIALS

From the time when man began living in permanent shelters we have had walls made from natural materials, ranging from the rough stone of a cave to the wattle-and-daub structure of a hut and the clay brick of a house. These days our treatment of natural wall coverings is more sophisticated, but the materials are much the same, from veneers of polished granite and stone to wooden panelling in tongue and groove.

We enjoy having natural materials in our home not only because they provide a link with the outdoors and nature, but also because of the infinite variety of pattern, colour and texture that can be found in them, from the rich red of cherry wood to the deep black of ebony, and from the brilliant

green of a Connemara marble to the snowy whiteness of Carrara or the matt greyness of slate. Natural materials also have a tactile quality, from the cool, smoothness of stone to the warm, graininess of wood.

The versatility of these materials has also been an important factor in their prolonged use in the home. Stone can be used on floors, worktops and sink surrounds as well as on walls, and wood can be used on those same surfaces but can be stained, polished, varnished or painted to give an infinite number of colours and finishes, depending on the desired effect.

Wooden panelling is a practical way to disguise uneven wall surfaces and to conceal remedial or structural amendments, it is also lighter and more versatile than stone when it comes to working around difficult angles or in awkward space. Because of its rigid composition stone is sometimes used in smaller sections such as mosaic or tile-sized pieces to cover uneven or irregular surfaces, and by cutting the stone into smaller sections you can create a mixed and more diverse arrangement of colour and pattern.

Although stone is very durable and needs little maintenance wood is susceptible to a number of problems. Natural wood that is protected by a varnish or wax finish may become marked if it comes into contact with hot or damp objects, but these marks can generally be treated and repaired. Wood will also swell if left in contact with water for a prolonged period, so it is not ideal for a bathroom, and excess heat will cause it to shrink and crack if has not been properly kiln dried and prepared before use.

ABOVE LEFT The honey colour of this pine panelling gives a feeling of warmth to the room; its natural grain, along with the lateral lines of the planks, provide pattern. Wood is also a good insulator of heat and noise.

ABOVE RIGHT Wood mellows and ages and takes on a patina that adds to its interest. Here broad planks have been used to create vertical panelling – because the joins run from the floor to the ceiling they enhance the feeling of height.

OPPOSITE Certain woods, such as tulip and walnut, have distinct grain configurations and rich reddish hues that create interesting wall facings. Fine wood veneers are invaluable for this because they are more malleable and less expensive than solid wood.

Three rows of a bright
orange tile form a dramatic
splashback in a white
kitchen and provide an
easy-to-wipe surface above
a food preparation area.

using coloured tiles

- Grade tiles from dark through to light to make an ombré or shadow effect.

- Make a chequerboard pattern of black and white or two tones of one colour for an impressive design.

- Coloured grout can be applied between plain white tiles to bring an unexpected element of colour.

Tiles are a practical wall or floor covering for any area where water is used often and in quantity, because well-laid and grouted tiles are water resistant and easy to clean. Tiles are often used in bathrooms and kitchens, where as well as being durable they can be colourful and decorative, whether in a block of colour, a pattern or pictorial mural.

Bathrooms and kitchens are areas associated with the need for hygiene so select crisp, clean colours that pschycologically endorse this – washes of colour or pale, white-based shades such as primrose, aquamarine, mint green and pale blue. You can use a slim border of tiles to separate an area of wall painted in one colour from another tiled in an opposing or complementary colour.

ABOVE By mixing various shades of mosaic tiles you can create a random design that is more visually stimulating than solid colour. The small tiles counterbalance the large squares of slate used on the main wall and sills.

RIGHT These scale-like tiles have tonal variations and glazed surfaces which reflect the light at different angles and intensity, making the surface interesting.

RIGHT The colour of the walls has been perfectly matched with the curtain fabric so that when the floor-length curtains are drawn the window area blends into the walls.

LEFT The deep red used on the shelf recess makes a striking contrast both to the pale blue walls of the room in the foreground and to the collection of white ceramics on display.

PAINTED WALLS

The key to a well-painted wall is in the ground work, the unseen preparation which takes time and patience. Plaster walls and panelling all require filling and sanding to achieve a smooth finish. Freshly applied and dried plaster and new wood may also need a base or sealing coat of paint to prevent the decorative top layer from sinking into the surface in an uneven fashion. A ground coat of paint will also help to bring out the full richness and intensity of the top coat of your chosen colour.

If the wall has previously been painted in a dark colour and you wish to change it to a lighter shade you will need to blank out or conceal the dark colour with a ground coat of white or pale paint. The opposite is also true – if the walls have been white and you want to paint them a rich dark colour you need a grey or dark-coloured base coat to provide a suitable surface on which to apply the deeper colour if you do not want white to show through.

Painted walls can be in a single colour framed by a contrasting skirting board and door surround, or you could try a paint effect. The most simple is a broad, repeating stripe; this can be accomplished by measuring out the stripe and masking the edges on either side with tape. Paint within the tape and when the paint is dry, peel off the tape and you should have a perfectly clean straight line. Another option is decorative squares or boxes which can be achieved using a similar technique with masking tape.

Stencils have been popular through the centuries; these can be made by cutting out a shape or motif in hardboard or stiff card then stippling paint through the outline and on to the wall. You could also try making a raised motif by cutting into a block of soft wood such as balsa, and pressing the raised area into a dish of paint before stamping it on the wall.

Other more elaborate decorative paint finishes can be traced back to Georgian and Victorian homes, when homeowners wanted the appearance of expensive marbles or richly grained wood but couldn't afford them, so had their walls skilfully painted to resemble these finishes.

There are also textural paint finishes where a dry steel comb is pulled through a thick top coat of paint; where the teeth of the comb drag the paint away the under-surface colour is revealed. Another effect is sponging, in which a damp sponge is applied to the surface of the paint while it is still wet and the paint is lifted away, leaving a mottled appearance.

ABOVE A complex linear pattern like this is built up in layers, starting with the broad bands and repetitive colours and finishing with the thin chocolate brown highlight feature.

LEFT Broad painted bands of colour, incorporating the shelf above the bed, make a big impression in a small bedroom and can be easily applied using a plumb line and masking tape.

OPPOSITE This painted frieze and ceiling are sensational and also help to make the room feel more intimate. If these areas had been painted in the same colour as the walls the room would have appeared cold, empty and blank.

The areas of recessed background and raised edging catch the light in different ways. The physical composition of panelling will naturally create areas of light and shade and subtle colour variation.

Decorative panelling

- When applying beading, punch the pin head below the surface of the wood and cover the hole with filler for a flawless finish.

- You can fake panelling on a plain plaster wall by gluing on moulding or architrave.

- If used in a bathroom, wood panelling should be painted with vinyl or gloss paint to make it water resistant.

Panelling has a number of useful aspects, it can be used to insulate and add warmth to a home and to disguise uneven or damaged wall surfaces, but panelling can also be used to exaggerate the height of a room, making it appear taller than it really is. This is achieved by creating tall slim outlines in beading which will take the eye upwards and exaggerate the height of the walls.

The inside of a panel is a useful place to apply a small quantity of an expensive paper, or to introduce a contrasting or highlight colour to a scheme. If you have found exquisite wallpaper but it is too expensive to use on a whole wall, create framed panels where a smaller amount of the paper can be used and shown to its best advantage.

ABOVE Oblong panels can be used to create an impression of height, and intricate beadwork adds to the overall grandeur.

RIGHT By varying the direction of the grain of the wood or veneer you can create unusual and interesting patterns.

RIGHT This grass-faced wallpaper is textured, which gives it a subtle vertical stripe and a raised surface. Similar papers can be covered in threads of raw silk, raffia or hemp fibres.

OPPOSITE The subtle, pearlized paisley pattern breaks up the intensity of the main colour and the shiny finish reflects light on the matt background.

BELOW A single wall of patterned wallpaper is used to bring together a number of elements – the brown of the wood panelling, the off-white of the walls and the floral pattern on the bed linen.

WALLPAPER

Once only a hand-painted luxury, machine-printed wallpapers now make these decorative coverings available to all. There are two basic categories of wallpapers, the plain and the highly decorative. Plain papers look similar to a painted finish with just a subtle grading of colour or a simple stripe or pattern, but they basically fulfil the same visual role as a painted wall.

Highly decorative papers are printed with a dense pattern, something too complex and detailed for an average person to be able to paint on to a wall. These papers are most frequently used on one wall or in a feature panel, because to decorate a whole room in them would create a claustrophobic atmosphere and also make the room seem smaller and overcrowded. To hang wallpaper successfully does require some skill and ground work. The wall surface must be smooth and

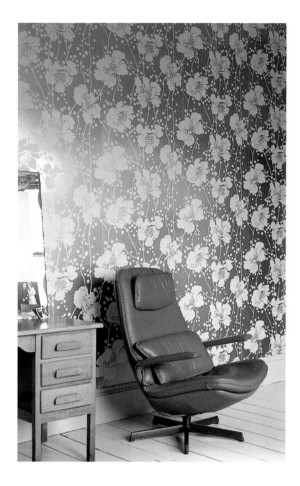

clean and to ensure that the paper hangs in a straight line use a plumb line. Patterns must be matched so that there is an uninterrupted run of the design from one drop to the next, and you must take this into account when estimating how much paper you will need.

You may also find wallpaper borders a useful way to introduce areas of colour; these narrow strips of decorative paper can be used to create the impression of a panel, picture or dado rail and may be used to bring an element of pattern to a plainly painted wall.

OPPOSITE In this large dining room the red of the wallpaper creates a cosy and relaxing atmosphere. The subtle lotus print breaks up the large expanse of colour and alludes to an oriental theme.

ABOVE For years it was popular to paint woodwork white, but in modern homes there is a movement to colour. Here the blue of the floral wallpaper is echoed in the skirting.

RIGHT Some of the most exclusive wallpapers are more like paintings than wall coverings and are often hand-painted rather than machine printed. This oriental-style paper is so dramatic and detailed that it requires little other embellishment or colour in the rest of the room.

ABOVE Rather than solid blocks of black and white these chequerboard squares have been made up using mosaics which, because of their smaller size, break up the density of the pattern and therefore reduce the strength of its impact.

FLOORS

A floor is the grounding part of any scheme; it is an area where contrast and colour can be introduced but it is also a place where a durable and resilient material is required.

NATURAL MATERIALS

As with natural wall coverings, natural flooring focuses mainly on stone and wood, although materials such as coir and bamboo are used, their fibres are generally woven into individual mats and runners or even fitted carpets.

Stone floor coverings come in a wide range of materials and palettes, from highly polished marble to sandstone and granite. The stone is generally cut into tile-like squares so that they are easier to lift and place and can be finished in a high-gloss polish or a more subdued matt effect. Stone floors are resilient and hardwearing, but fragile things will invariable break if dropped on them and the 'softer' materials such as slate may stain if oil or grease comes in to contact with its surface.

Hardwood flooring such as oak, in a variety of tones, can be laid in straight planks or in more decorative patterns such as parquet herringbone, chevron or basket weave and borders may be added using a contrasting darker coloured wood such as walnut, maple or Wenge.

Wood may also be stained, so that an inexpensive pine can appear the colour of rich mahogany or walnut, but wood must be sealed with a protective finish such as varnish, wax or oil, which must be regularly stripped and replenished to maintain a durable and attractive surface.

This arrangement of floor tiles has been carefully laid so that those under the stools, which will be pulled backwards and forwards under the table, are smooth. Those in the main walk through traffic area have a more coarse and textured surface.

CARPETS AND RUGS

Carpets and rugs are an effective way of introducing colour to a room. If the walls are plain or in a low-key shade the floor is an ideal area on which to place a panel or block of colour. Because the carpet or rug is rarely seen in its entirety — being partially hidden beneath seats or tables - its full impact is reduced, therefore you can afford to select a more vibrant or daring colour than you might otherwise choose for other surfaces in the room.

A colourful rug creates a visual focus, especially in an openplan living room, where it can be used to define or delineate a certain area. For example, in an openplan living room where there are kitchen, dining and sitting

ABOVE In a room where windows dominate and there is little wall space, the floor may be the major area to display colour and pattern. There are many vintage-style rugs being manufactured to complement the classic furniture designs of the mid-20th century, so you can create a scheme that has period style.

spaces, the dining and sitting zones can be separated and outlined by placing the relevant furniture on large rugs in different colours. Rugs and carpets also offer an opportunity to balance a scheme. For example, if the overall appearance of your room is light and white then a deeper or darker toned carpet can act as a grounding element, forming a base to the scheme. Conversely, if the room is predominantly dark then a light shade of carpet will help to give it a lift and help to prevent a feeling of oppression.

There are a number of carpet companies that will custom make rugs to suit your colour scheme and floor area, and there is a growing interest in 'jigsaw' carpets made up of several shapes or strips of colour that can be used as single entities or joined together to form a whole.

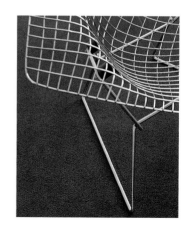

ABOVE RIGHT A plain-coloured carpet will create a solid surface of colour that is a good background to streamlined or fine-framed furniture.

BELOW If you have an awkward or difficult space to fill with a rug you could create your own using a length of standard carpet with bound edges, or commission one to be made to a specific size.

Black painted floors and
white walls are a classic
and stylish combination,
against which any period or
type of furniture can be set.
Old or damaged wooden
floors can be revitalized
with a couple of coats of
hardwearing paint or stain.

PAINTED FLOORS

Painted floors are usually wooden, and can be a good way of disguising a well-worn or distressed floor, giving it a new lease of life. Painted floors can be tinted with just a wash of colour, such as the bleaching and lightening effect of limewash, or they can be completely concealed under coats of thick gloss russet red, black, white or chocolate brown paint. If a wash of colour is used the floor should be sealed afterwards with a matt or gloss varnish to provide some protection to the painted surface.

Painted floors, especially in paler shades, will need to be frequently washed to maintain a crisp clean appearance, and because of wear and tear under foot they may need to be stripped and repainted from time to time.

Painted floors can also be found in patterns, but most often the designs are geometric such as squares or stripes. On natural wood floors painted borders, often in a simple pattern such as the Greek Key, can be painted to resemble the types of inlay found in more expensive wooden floors.

Painted floors provide a perfect background to runners and rugs, and can be decorated in colours to highlight the pattern and tones of the carpet or to contrast with it. Hallways and staircases are areas where this treament can be particularly successful, when this combination of flooring is used.

BELOW LEFT A high-gloss white floor will reflect light and brighten a dark room, but it is a difficult surface to maintain because it shows every scuff and mark. There are a number of poured rubber alternatives that will achieve a similar effect but be more practical in a family home.

BELOW RIGHT The colour of some natural wood floors can be too intense or vivid for a pale room scheme, but the floor can be sanded, to remove the varnish or seal, and then white-washed or limed to reduce the strength of the colour.

LEFT These light voile curtains help to soften the angular and grid-like lines of the floor-to-ceiling windows, but they do not reduce the flow of light or block the view. Red fabric ties tone with the upholstered dining chairs.

RIGHT Two layers of curtains can be used to great effect. The finer voiles will reduce the impact of strong sunlight while the circle-printed outer curtains will give a feeling of warmth and comfort when drawn at night.

FABRICS

Fabrics come in a multitude of colours, patterns and textures. They can be dyed to match wall and other surface shades exactly or be the main point of the most vivid and notable contrast in a room.

CURTAINS AND BLINDS

Window dressings form two functions in a room. One is to control and direct the flow of light and the other is to add to the decorative scheme, and you can use these functions alone or together. A light voile or blind will control the flow of light during the day and obscure the view, as well as providing a certain amount of privacy, while the secondary layer of a more formal 'dress' curtain can be drawn at night to shut out the dark and create a more cosy and intimate atmosphere in the room, as well as to enhance and contribute to the colour scheme and decorative ambience.

Blinds and lightweight curtains such as voiles are usually in white, off-white or a pale colour so that the quality of the daylight that filters through them remains unadulterated, but decorative or coloured voiles are a way of enhancing a colour scheme – the light that shines through will appear tinted, adding to the intensity of colour in the room.

Venetian blinds may be vertical or horizontal and come in a range of colours and decorative patterns as well as metallic finishes. They are often used when there is little space for a pole or curtain track; the blinds can be fitted within the recess.

In dress curtains the finish or type of material used is as important as the colour. A dark velvet will absorb light whereas a reflective surface such as silk or satin will reflect it and influence the way colour is perceived.

ABOVE Fine voiles can be used to reduce the glare at windows that get the full morning sun, but they are also useful for obscuring an unattractive view. Here the colour of the voile has been chosen to complement the walls.

LEFT Curtains don't have to be solid pieces of a single fabric; the main colour has been broken up with inset bands of cream and grey that echo the tones used in the wallpaper and on the chair.

OPPOSITE With certain styles of curtains a pelmet is added at the top of the window to frame the drapes and disguise the pole or track. This pelmet matches the curtains, but it could equally have been finished in the plain pink or beige fabric used on the sofa.

The two lavender throws draped over the backs and seats of the chairs in front of the window make the white chairs noticeable against the white background, and also emphasize their symmetry.

Using coloured throws

- Lightweight kelims, soft silk carpets and animal skins can all be used as throws to drape over the back of a sofa or chair.

- Throws are a simple way of lifting the monotony of a single-coloured duvet or bedcover, adding interest.

- You can have throws specially made, using the same colour and design of fabric that has featured elsewhere in the room.

Throws are an embellishment, although they can be useful in covering up a worn sofa back or arm or for snuggling under on a cool winter night. In decorating terms, their primary purpose is to pick up on colour and add to the overall appearance of a piece of furniture.

Throws can be made from any material that drapes and folds – they can be luxurious in fur-like fabrics or a simple woollen blanket. Some may be double sided so that they are more versatile. For example, one side may be in rough linen while the other side is smooth cashmere, or the throw may be in two colours, either contrasting or in a dark and light shade of the same colour. By changing the side of the throw on show you can bring a subtle change in mood or colour emphasis.

ABOVE Small throws can both protect the arms and backs of pale-coloured furniture and inject a shot of colour.

RIGHT A plain white bedcover looks clean and fresh, but on a large bed it can look bland. This simple deep pink throw lifts and defines the bed and makes it a feature of the room.

RIGHT The different black-and-white striped cushions attract the eye to the otherwise dark and subdued sofa on which they are arranged.

BELOW Cushion covers are limited in area so they are the perfect place to display a small, rare or expensive remnant of fabric. Here ornate metallic thread panels have been set as a band across plain silk cushions.

OPPOSITE A couple of cushions in ethnic fabric instantly set the mood of this room. They form a link with the carvings on the sideboard and the collection of tribal stools in the foreground.

CUSHIONS

Cushions are an easy and effective way to introduce colour and pattern in any scheme. They are small and easily swapped or rearranged to create different emphasizes of colours. Cushion covers are simple to remove and replace so that for a small amount of effort and expense you could bring a seasonal change to your room, using richer darker colours for a cosy winter appearance and lighter fresher colours in the summer.

Cushions also provide a surface where you can introduce small amounts of brilliant and bold pattern and texture, picking up on the main colours of your theme and mixing them with others. For example, a sofa upholstered in a roughly textured tweedy mix of green and browns will be a good foil to cushions in a solid gold chenille cover, a brightly striped green and orange silk and a coffee brocade or damask. The richness of the cushions will reduce the rustic roughness of the tweed but pick up the colours in its composition.

You can also vary the shapes and sizes of cushions, from sausage-shaped bolsters and round shapes to classic squares in a range of sizes, which again will create interest and variety. You can use modestly sized cushions as a way of displaying a small amount of an expensive or vintage fabric that might not be affordable or available in more substantial amounts.

The subtle stripe in the fabric of the wall hanging makes it stand out against the plain background and also helps focus attention on the pale-toned, dark-framed sketches.

Wall hangings

- If the fabric is light, the bottom edge might need to be weighted to keep it taut and straight.

- Attach a hanging to a pole either by making a stitched fold at the top, through which the pole can pass, or use large metal rings which can slide over the pole.

- You can finish the ends of the pole with a decorative finial or knob if you prefer.

Wall hangings date back to medieval times when they were used in the homes of the wealthy as a form of decoration. Nowadays, they are used in contemporary homes in much the same way as a panel of decorative wallpaper. Hangings can be framed or bordered in black or a rich contrasting colour to bring out the colour within the hanging, and to make it stand out against the wall on which it is diaplayed.

Wall hangings are usually banner-style and suspended from a pole or rod fixed at the top of a wall. As well as artwork-style wall hangings fabric can be hung at dado rail height to provide a decorative backdrop and some protection to the wall, especially if it is painted in a chalky paint wash that might brush off against clothing.

ABOVE A series of bright geometric-patterned ethnic cloths are used to enliven a narrow entrance hall.

RIGHT This wall hanging creates a focal point in part of the sitting area, a useful device in any openplan living space, where several functions can take place in one room.

RIGHT These rococo-style chairs have a silvered frame that complements the deep blue upholstery and the button-back detail. The decoratively carved arms and legs are balanced by the simplicity of the fabric.

BELOW The boxy shape of this contemporary sofa and recliner fits comfortably into the corner of the room. Its simple, single colour upholstery is lifted with a throw and two layers of tone-on-tone cushions.

FURNITURE

The period style and shape of an item of furniture can be a useful indicator as to the colours and patterns that suit its shape, but when in doubt go for a plain fabric rather than a densely patterned one. Plain colours make an object less dominating and can help to reduce a bulky appearance.

UPHOLSTERED

Upholstered furniture usually comprises the larger pieces in a room – the armchairs, sofas and perhaps a footstool – so their presence is dominant and therefore important. Although traditionally these items were together classified as a suite, often three-piece, and covered in matching fabric, the modern trend is to mix and match fabrics or to cover one piece in a dramatic or bold colour so that it becomes what is known as a 'statement' piece.

Patterned fabrics are often favoured for upholstery because any stain, mark or area of wear is less obvious, whereas on a plain fabric these blemishes would be more noticeable. But with modern stain-repellent fabric finishes or the option of removable, washable covers, plain coloured upholstered furniture is increasingly popular as a smart decorating choice.

The overstuffed style and squashy shape of this sofa is inviting, and the red of the covers adds to the feelings of warmth and comfort that it imparts. Because the walls are white they balance the heat and dramatic impact of this vibrant piece of furniture.

Where upholstered furniture is arranged in pairs, as in matching sofas on either side of a fireplace or a pair of armchairs near a coffee table, it is usual to cover them in the same fabric, whereas if you have an odd or single chair it is the best candidate for an alternative or different fabric covering.

Another concept seen in modern homes is to upholster the body of the sofa in one material but to cover the cushions in something contrasting, for example, the back and base of the sofa or armchair could be covered with a hardwearing black fabric while the cushions are dressed in a dramatic black and white floral print. In most cases these cushion covers are removable so could be replaced with a black and red stripe or plain material for a change.

ABOVE The colour of the material used on the seats and inner surfaces of this sofa is compatible with the natural woven basketwork of the outer facings. The sofa, on tall slim legs, is also visually delicate, so the pale yellow enhances the appearance of lightness and refinement.

BELOW The chequerboard effect of the black and white upholstery on the sofa mimics the grid of the window panes on the wall behind. The impact of the check is balanced by the addition of the blue footstool and lime green chairs, which provide a counterpoint to the monochrome pattern.

RIGHT The olive green upholstery of the sofa picks up on the sludgy tone of the floor covering and the charcoal grey of the chair and stair balustrades, but also defines it as an object in its own right.

With stand-alone seating, for example a designer recliner chair or vintage piece, it is advisable to play down pattern and concentrate on the colour of the upholstery. This is especially true when dealing with graceful or complex lines where the shape and style should be admired, rather than the fabric.

For a more standard seat you can use colour to add to its visual impact; for example, on an average armchair plain covers can be enhanced with contrast piping. Try lifting a red upholstered cushion with white piping or a white cover with navy piping: these simple but effective devices will accentuate the outline and can make a dull piece of furniture eye-catching.

Certain styles of chair have specific types of covering; for example, the classic Charles Eames chair and ottoman are invariably seen in black leather upholstery. If you are re-upholstering vintage or classic furniture it is worth looking up relevant archive material to see in which fabric or material the original design was finished, as a point of reference.

OPPOSITE The furniture here is predominantly wooden, linking with the staircase and providing a warm, natural-hued earthiness to a room that is open and sparely decorated.

BELOW Covered in plain red, white and black fabrics, the furniture keeps the colour palette simple, while the textures of the rug, white fake-fur upholstered chair and the mirrored artwork panel create the interest in the scheme.

By using a small, rather than full-length, back cushion on the bench seat the proportion of red, and therefore its impact, is reduced. The orange chair and footstool in front have an element of red in their composition so are compatible, although tonally different.

LEFT Sometimes the shape or style of a chair is a statement in itself, so needs little in the way of assistance from colour or fabric. The dark frames of these canopy-topped chairs are accentuated by the vivid yellow of the cushions and pads.

RIGHT Traditionally, dining chairs are all upholstered in the same fabric. Chairs with well-padded seats and backs are the most comfortable seating on which to spend a prolonged period at table.

TABLES AND CHAIRS

Tables are usually made from wood, metal, glass or moulded resin or plastic, or a combination of these materials, so it is the cloths and things upon them, such as glass and ceramic vases, that can bring colour to a room. Although wooden tables can be stained or painted and resin or plastic tables, usually smaller rather than larger, are available in a range of colours, it is rarely the table itself that makes a colourful impact on its own.

As with cushions and throws, table mats, runners and cloths can be replaced to change the colour focus of the room or on a dining table to complement the china, glassware or theme of the meal you are serving. For example, if your meal has an Italian theme a red and white check cloth or red, white and green table mats can accentuate it, or if the meal is based on seafood a simple blue cloth could allude to the idea of the sea.

Dining chairs and other freestanding upright seats often have a softening seat pad, which can be covered in a colourful, decorative fabric, and some dining chairs are dressed with semi-fitted, floor-length covers which give a more formal appearance. This can be in a colour that complements the table dressing or other aspects of the room. These covers can be tailored to suit the occasion, from a cream calico for informal events to rich red brocade embellished with braid for grand affairs.

CUPBOARDS AND STORAGE

It seems that there is never enough storage in the modern home for the clutter our complex lifestyles seem to attract. Increasingly, valuable living space is being enclosed in cupboards or divided by shelves to accommodate this paraphernalia, and so their colour treatment is very important.

Built-in cupboards are either painted to blend in with the main wall colour or they can provide an opportunity to introduce a different tone or colour, therefore becoming a feature in their own right. With doors that blend in, or surfaces that have been painted with a pattern or decorative finish, unseen opening devices such as a concealed or press latch ensure that the face of the door is smooth and uninterrupted by handles or knobs.

Shelves are another area of storage that can benefit from an injection of colour. By painting shelves in a contrasting colour to the wall they become a feature, whereas painting them to match the wall will make the objects on them appear to hang in space. You can also paint the underside of a shelf to give a subtle glimpse of colour when you are sitting down.

Freestanding units such as chests of drawers and armoires can be painted to match a room, or to pick up on a feature colour. In a technique seen in much Swedish furniture they can be decorated to highlight the shape or features, so that the drawers and top are outlined in a darker shade of the main colour.

LEFT To break up the monotony of large areas of identical units, patterned paper or fabric can be fixed to the panel sections of the doors. Here the palette of colours is based on the primaries - red, blue and yellow.

RIGHT In a room otherwise void of features, such as in a kitchen where surface areas are best left free of clutter, you can introduce colour in the storage units. Here sliding doors in coloured Perspex make a bright impact.

RIGHT The graded colours of these glass vessels encourages the eye to follow through the arrangement. Green, a secondary colour made from yellow and blue, is always compatible with yellow elements.

OPPOSITE The juxtaposition of the small dishes and large vase with the glass bird emphasizes the common colour of blue, but also contrasts the delicacy of the bird with the solidity of the ceramics.

BELOW The pleats in the curtain and ribbing on the base of the table are picked up in the linear pattern of the stylized jug, so there is a theme running through this cameo. The dark blue of the taller vase separates the jug in front of it from the curtain of the same shade.

ACCESSORIES

Glass and china are made in a myriad of colours so there is always a good possibility of finding a piece or pieces that perfectly match your scheme, no matter how unusual and off-beat your choice of colours might be.

Arrangements of colourful china and glass will increase the visual stimulus in your room and can be used to reinforce highlighted or accent colours. For example, in a mainly grey sitting room a vase or collection of ceramic bowls in a primary colour will be a focus of attention. On a shelf against a beige wall a group of highly decorated and gilded china figures or vessels will be noticeable, but arrangements must be limited and well displayed otherwise your room may take on the appearance of a junk shop.

Grouping is an important part of how objects are viewed. Odd numbers are more interesting than even, so groups of three, five or seven objects are preferable. Try to arrange objects of varying sizes so that the eye is taken up to a central high point. You can also layer displays so that larger darker pieces are in the background and smaller lighter coloured objects are in front.

LEFT A strong wall colour can help bring cohesion to an arrangement of diverse shapes or many colours. This rich terracotta wall shows up the delicate weaving and natural colour of the straw baskets, while subduing the exuberance of the African headdress above.

RIGHT Three small ceramic vessels not only define the corner of the transparent glass table, but also echo the colour of the footstool behind, making the impact of red in the scheme much more notable.

You can highlight and define a specific favourite colourful object by placing it on a mat or coloured base. For example, a collection of fine white porcelain vases may be lost in a pale-coloured room, but by placing the vases on a red or vibrant-coloured mat they will become more noticeable. Transparent objects such as glass can benefit from being placed against a coloured background or on a base of a different colour, and in some cases a mirror can be effective as it reflects the object as well as the available natural light, so giving the glass objects a further level of highlight.

Lighting is a useful tool when it comes to displaying objects, especially when a dark object is placed against a wall in a deep colour. Glass and china as well as paintings and artworks can be illuminated by individual electrical task lights which focus the beam, and therefore the eye, on the object.

Because decorative glass and ceramic accessories are arranged to be objects of interest and to complement your colour scheme they must be kept in pristine condition, therefore frequently washed and polished. They can then be rearranged or placed in different locations so that the display is never static and is of fresh interest each time you come into the room.

colourful spaces

One of the cardinal rules of design is to make a space fit its purpose, and in decorative terms this could be interpreted as choosing colours that are appropriate to the particular use of the room. If you have a bright sunlit kitchen and you decorate it in vibrant red and orange the room will feel hot even before you turn on the oven or hob, and rapidly become uncomfortable once you start to cook. But if you use a panel of muted red, teamed with lots of stainless steel surfaces and perhaps the earthiness of walnut or cherry wood, you will create a cooler, calmer and more productive environment.

The direction a room faces will affect the penetration and quality of light available and therefore the way colour is seen and experienced. As well as the light levels, there are also associations connected with the compass points so, for example, a room that faces north is said to have an outlook on the direction of maturity, south represents simplicity, east youthfulness and the west ageing. The associations of east and west may reflect the fact that the sun rises or is 'born' in the east, while it sets in the west, at the end of the day when it has 'aged', so the direction of a room may also influence the activity or use that is carried out there. For example, a bedroom could benefit from facing east as the morning sun will invigorate and make it easier to get out of bed, whereas a cool, north-facing room will make you want to stay under the bedclothes. Clever use of colour can manipulate these associations in a positive way.

TOP LEFT The use of wood on the floor and folding screen, and the tanned leather upholstery of the armchairs, create a scheme that focuses on shades of brown.

TOP RIGHT Small amounts of colour can have a big impact. In a room where there is one or two pale or natural tones a panel of a primary colour will alter the mood and perspective of the space.

BELOW LEFT A black and white monochrome scheme will focus the eye on details and textures, such as the recess filled with logs and the delicate glass pendant chandelier.

BELOW RIGHT Colour can be used sparingly but effectively. Here the shades of black, white and grey are combined in a bold check, which makes a memorable impression in this striking bedroom.

PREVIOUS PAGES Against a bright white background, and with ample natural light in this room, it is good to use strong vibrant colours for the upholstery of the furniture. If pale colours or white had been selected the furniture could easily have been lost in the space.

LIVING ROOMS

A living room is generally regarded as the most public space in a home, where strangers as well as friends and family may be greeted or entertained. This room is also a place for rest and relaxation, where people of all ages may congregate, so when choosing colours for its decoration you need to take all these diverse aspects into consideration.

There are a number of options for a scheme for a sitting room. The most common choice is the 'Safe Palette' based on off-whites, shades that have a white base with just a hint of colour. These provide a neutral background against which all other contrast or highlight colours work.

The living room, on frequent display, gives a visitor an insight into your personal space and therefore your personality. Some people choose to decorate with the 'Fashionable Palette', picking up on colours and trends that are in vogue and seen on the pages of interiors magazines, therefore conveying the impression of someone who is up to date with current trends.

FAR LEFT This simple overall scheme is made up of black, white and beige, but is made notable by the inclusion of modern zebra print upholstery on the two period-style chairs and the circle artwork over the fireplace. Without these two features the room could have been bland.

THIS PAGE The use of pattern – stripes on the sofa and a repeated fleur-de-lis design on the armchair – brings interest to this muted, low-key palette. The four-fold screen emphasizes the blue composition of the fabric prints.

A third option is the 'Shared Palette' most often found in a family home. The 'Shared Palette' is where different styles and colour preferences are brought together to make a single scheme that is acceptable to the two or more parties who inhabit the space. 'Shared Palettes' are usually complex to devise, but can result in unusual and interesting mixes.

Finally there is the 'Mixed Palette'. This is where diverse objects, fabrics, furniture and textures are brought together by a common or compatible colour – the result is usually a bohemian look, but it can be given cohesion and stability if one or two main colours are selected and featured. For example, a strong colour such as red or black will provide a background to prints, paintings, wall hangings and ethnic artefacts, allowing the colours and patterns of the individual objects to stand out but not overpower the room.

Another consideration when planning a scheme, especially for a living room, is that if you are making a particular statement or conveying a certain style, be sure that it is obvious. If your strategy is for something to be, for example, green then ensure that it is there in strength and volume. There is no use being timid, especially with a strong or vibrant colour – you need to have the strength of your convictions to get the message across.

The living room is also the place where you will have static and movable elements of colour. The static will be the fixed surfaces, such as solid walls or panels of colour, the floor and the ceiling, and the movable ones will be single chairs, cushions, throws and accessories.

ABOVE LEFT A simple muted scheme such as this would provide a perfect backdrop for seasonal accessory change. You could add zesty lime cushions and throws in the summer and similar accessories in warm rust and amber tones for the winter.

ABOVE RIGHT Large pieces of furniture such as these ample armchairs benefit from being upholstered in mid and light tones, which will help to make them appear less dominant in a small room. If they were covered in a hot red or black fabric they would be overpowering.

OPPOSITE Be bold with your colour choices. Once you have chosen your colour theme – in this case variations on shades of dusky purple – be prepared to carry that choice through the whole space.

The movable decorative elements in a space may be used to create a contrast or point of interest against those that are fixed. For example, if you have a pale floor or wall colour a single stool or seat with a brightly coloured cushion could be positioned so as to break up the expanse of a single colour. On a large area of dark floor a light rug will have the same effect. Cushions and throws are the easiest and most versatile way of introducing a different tone or breaking up a large plane of a single colour (see more about the practical use of throws and cushions on pages 80-83).

Practical considerations may also play a part in your choice of colour, especially for upholstered furniture. In a family home large sofas, used for lounging and sitting and sometimes as a trampoline, are best covered in removable and washable covers, especially if you opted for a pale shade. A fixed cover will be more durable in a dark colour, preferable treated with a stain resistant finish. For day to day protection you could add a coloured throw or tab-tied cover, which will offer some protection against regular family use.